Navigation Workbook
for
Practice Underway

The next step beyond textbook and classroom

David Burch and Larry Brandt

STARPATH

Seattle, WA

ISBN 978-0-914025-47-4

Published by

Starpath Publications

3050 NW 63rd Street, Seattle, WA 98107

Manufactured in the United States of America

www.starpathpublications.com

Contents

Overview and Instructions

This Workbook will serve as your menu of practice exercises and logbook for onboard navigation training, either on your own or as part of a group. Please skim through it to see what is covered. Once you know what is here, you will always have some navigation exercise to work on if you like. During an onboard course this provides navigation practice even when the instructor is working with other crew members at the moment. At the end of the voyage, it will be your documentation and souvenir of the voyage.

The goal is to work as many of these exercises each day as your time and interest permits. Some may require reviewing the topic from your reference materials, but after that you have the forms to carry out more examples on your own. Some exercises you can work alone, others you can share with other crew members.

There is no order to the projects. Just take whatever project might be convenient at the time, or choose ones related to the day's discussions. In a sense this is serendiptiy practice. We are not getting the exercises from a book but from what we happen to be confronted with in our travels. The order of the projects within individual sections corresponds roughly to the complexity of the exercise. The exercises are grouped in subject headings, although many are interrelated.

For most exercises, the first thing to record is the Date, Time, and Position. You get the latter from the chart or the nearest GPS position. Record both Lat-Lon and a brief text description, ie 1.5 mi SW of Point Sheridan. In most cases, Lat-Lon to the nearest tenth of a minute will be adequate, ie 47° 34.6' N. That corresponds to about ±600 feet, which is all that is needed. In a few cases, when more accurate specification might be useful, use 34.56, which is about ±60 ft, or even 34.563 which is about 6 ft, however none of the instrumentation will be that accurate, but it can indeed be more accurate than 60 ft.

Some of these exercises are very basic and quick, others will take more time. In either case, it will be instructive to record your results, not just do them. You will want to document what has been covered.

There is always the possibility to learn many things on any extended voyage, so we need some way to organize what we have done so we can be most effective with the time we have. The entry will document when you actually did the exercises and what is left to do. This is also true for your own general sailing. If you keep a written record of navigation experiences (separate from the ship's log) you gain local knowledge at a much faster rate than just relying on memory alone. This Workbook is designed for those records.

You may want to practice some of them on scratch paper before entering in this book, or use pencil, so if an exercise gets started that does not get finished, you can erase it. Also for some of them, you may want more detailed records than there are places in the forms, in which case there is often extra space on the pages. When using a separate notebook, if you label your notes such as GPS-1 on May 22, for example, you will be able to correlate notebook and Workbook.

Also note a few exercises take some time to complete, involving a longer run, with data gathered at the beginning and end only, or only periodically throughout the day, in which case you might be working on more than one at a time. Start a longer one, then if you like, work on others while the longer one is cooking.

Basic Chart Work

CW-1. Use of Chart Catalog

Refer to the appropriate nautical chart catalog to see what charts are available at your present location. Do this towards the beginning, middle, and end of the voyage. Record the chart number and scale of the largest-scale chart and the next smaller (2), ie at Port Townsend, WA in Catalog 2 we find 18474 at 1:25,000 as the most detailed and 18465 at 1:80,000 as the next one smaller. "Larger scale" means things are larger, ie more detailed. There might be a printed chart catalog on board, or this info can also be obtained from any of the electronic chart programs (select the option "show chart outlines"). See also downloadable version from links at www.starpath.com/getcharts.

Date	Location along voyage	Chart w. largest scale	Chart w. next scale down
7/20/15	Port Townsend	18474, 1:25,000	18465, 1:80,000

References:

Inland & Coastal Navigation, 2nd Ed. Chapter 2, Sections 2.1, 2.2

CW-2. Lat/Lon, Range and Bearings

For any chart onboard, mark any two points in the water that are about one or two outstretched hand spans apart. Read the Lat and Lon of the two points and measure the distance between them (R in nmi), then the true bearing (B) from one to the other, and note the magnetic variation at the area of the marks. Do this at some point with a small scale chart (1:80,000 or greater) and also with a large scale chart (1:40,000 or smaller). Record the Lat/Lon to nearest 0.01' if you can. This will depend on the chart scale. [We will use these same points for CW-3 so make a small light mark in pencil on the chart so you can find them again easily.]

#	Date	Chart No / scale	Point 1 Lat/Lon	Point 2 Lat/Lon	R	B (T)	Var
1							
2							
3							
4							
5							
6							
7							
8							

References:

Inland & Coastal Navigation, 2nd Ed. Chapter 2, Sections 2.9, 2.10

CW-3. Depths and Soundings

For the examples worked in CW-2, record the depth units used for the chart (feet, fathoms, meters), then record the charted depths at the first and second points, interpolating between nearest soundings as needed. Then find the deepest water and shallowest water between the two points. Again, you may have to interpolate to get the answer. Have an instructor check your work at some point. Then look on the chart to find the value of Mean High Water (MHW) at the location of the points.

#	Date	Depth units	Depth at Point 1	Depth at Point 2	Deepest	Shallowest	MHW
1							
2							
3							
4							
5							
6							
7							
8							

References:

Inland & Coastal Navigation, 2nd Ed. Chapter 2, Sections 2.5, 2.7

CW-4. Buoys

On any coastwise voyage we rely much on buoys to confirm our route. There are many types of buoys with different meanings. The main reference for meaning is the chart, from which it is usually apparent what a buoy marks. For more information see the USCG and NIMA *Light Lists* which lists every buoy in the waterway and includes info not on the chart. Next is the booklet *Chart No. 1*, which gives a general description of what the chart symbols might mean. There will be copies of both books available for working these exercises.

Vector chart programs also include some *Light List* information on various aids to navigation. For each new type of buoy you observe, record the location, then use a Light List to find its official number—at which time you will learn more about the aid. Every light and buoy has a unique number. There is a US and International numbering system, plus tables that correlate the numbers. We have a separate exercise (CW-5) for Lighthouses, but you might include here prominent daymarks or beacons as well as buoys.

Date	Time	Lat/Lon	Buoy description	LL number	Chart – LL differences

References:

Inland & Coastal Navigation, 2nd Ed. Chapter 2, Sections 2.11, 2.13

CW-5. Lighthouses

What's a lighthouse? Let's just call them any prominent light in some prominent structure that sort of looks like a house. This is just a record of these key landmarks along the voyage. The main exercise is to use the Light List and compare the Light List description with the chart description. You can also use this form for any prominent light, even if it is not a lighthouse. *Read the discussion with CW-4 above.* We have another exercise (NR-3) where we record vessel lights. This is for permanent navigation lights.

Date	Time	Lat/Lon	Light description	LL number	Chart – LL differences

References:

Inland & Coastal Navigation, 2nd Ed. Chapter 2, Sections 2.11, 2.12

CW-6. Coast Pilots and Sailing Directions

The goal of the *Coast Pilots* is to present crucial navigation information that is not on the chart. These are important aids to any voyage. They are also referred to as *Sailing Directions* in Canada. There will be copies on board both in paper and as computer files. The latter have the advantage of being able to be quickly searched electronically, but they are not always convenient to access when you might need them. Ideally, every leg of a route that is new to you should be researched in the corresponding Sailing Directions ahead of time. There is always something interesting to learn.

Record here the sections that you have read relating to the present voyage, plus the name of the book. There are US versions for US waters, US versions for Canadian waters (as well as all other parts of the world) and there are excellent Canadian versions for their own waters. The British Admiralty also makes a very extensive (and very expensive) set for the world.

Date	Time	Region studied	Book title	Notes / Comments

References:

Inland & Coastal Navigation, 2nd Ed. Chapter 3, Sections 3.1, 3.2, 3.3

CW-7. Local Knowledge

Almost any lengthy coastal voyage benefits at some point from information gleaned from 'Local Knowledge'. List here instances of such opportunities that may occur on your voyage, and state the kind of knowledge received and how you might have benefitted.

Date	Location	Source	Nature of Knowledge or Advice	Benefit

References:

Inland & Coastal Navigation, 2nd Ed. Chapter 2, Section 2.4

Special Communications and AIS

COM-1. Securite', Pan Pan, and Mayday Communications

It is unusual that any long distance coastal voyage can be completed without hearing at least one of these special classes of radio communications. To remind ourselves of the importance of each of these, state in your own words or obtain from an onboard reference a definition of each as follows:

Class of Transmission	Description
Securite'	
Pan Pan	
Mayday	

If you hear such a radio call, list here the date, time and your vessel location, and indicate the class of transmission together with a summary of the message.

Date	Time	Your Location	Class	Message Summary

References:

Inland & Coastal Navigation, 2nd Ed. Chapter 3

COM-2. Broadcast Notice to Mariners

Charts are updated annually by the Light List, weekly by the printed Local Notices to Mariners, and daily by the Broadcast notice to mariners (as well as Internet). Underway, our most convenient source of up to date chart information as well as any other special announcement relevant to navigation is the Broadcast Notices given on USCG VHF channel 22. Schedules are usually on the marine weather services charts or might be found online. There are also Canadian counterparts.

Record here your examples of listening to these reports. Note whether the notices were labeled by the announcement as a Securite' or Pan Pan designation. They also repeat weather information, which can be a valuable supplement to the regular VHF weather broadcasts.

Date	Time	VHF channel / Station	Notes / Comments

References:

Emergency Navigation

COM-3. Automated Identification System

If your vessel is equipped with AIS of any class, whether Class-A, Class-B or Receive Only, obtain from onboard references information about it and place that information here. Indicate what transmitter power (if applicable) your vessel's AIS has, along with the type of display for received AIS targets (i.e. text, ECS display, dedicated plotter, Internet app.)

AIS Class	Ship MMSI	VHF Antenna Location	Transmitter Power (if Applicable)	AIS Display

COM-4. AIS Maximum Range

Different class AIS transceivers transmit their data at different power levels; therefore some AIS targets can be received from a quite long way away. Log here some sample AIS targets received at exceptional long distances (perhaps as much as 50 nmi distance):

Date	Time	Own Ship Location	Target Name	Target Location	Range & Bearing to AIS Target

AIS References:

navcen.uscg.gov/?pageName=AISmain , see also *Inland & Coastal Navigation, 2nd Ed.* Chapter 12, Section 12.19

COM-5. AIS Communication

The special benefit of AIS is the ability for an equipped vessel to identify another vessel by name even though both vessels may be out of direct line of sight. Being able to call a specific vessel by name enables bridge-to-bridge communications for important purposes, such as to negotiate the passing of vessels in potentially close quarter situations.

List here some instances where your voyage benefitted by another ship's calling you, or your calling them, based on information obtained through AIS even though you and they were not in direct line of sight. Indicate both vessels' locations, and summarize the purpose of the communication.

Date	Time	Own Ship Location	Target Vessel Name	Target Location	Range & Bearing to Vessel	Purpose of Communication

COM-6. Virtual & Synthetic Navaids

Pseudo-navigation aids broadcast via AIS ground stations are rapidly being implemented, promising enhancements to maritime safety as well as reduced costs to establish and maintain. If your vessel has an AIS receiver and a compatible method of displaying AIS targets, you may come across these special aids from time to time. Log them below as you come across them.

Virtual Navaids – these are navaids within the electronic AIS environment that are placed where no physical aid to navigation exists.

Date	Location	Navaid Name	Description	Light List Entry, if any

Synthetic Navaids – these are navaids within the electronic AIS environment that 'overlay' physical aids to navigation.

Date	Location	Navaid Name	Description	Light List Entry, if any

Tides and Currents

TC-1. Tides at Anchor

For one or more of our anchorages, record the depth from the depth sounder, then compare that with the charted depth and the predicted tides for that location. You will need to know the "draft" of the transducer, which can be learned from the skipper, and you will need to use whatever tide source you have. There are books on board with tide height information, or they can be obtained even more easily from the electronic chart program.

This will also give practice on interpolating the tide tables, but if you use the computer, you can find it directly at the exact time you care about. The "Error" list in the table is the difference between measured water depth plus draft and the charted depth plus the present value of the tide for your location and time. Error = Sum 1 – Sum 2, or vice versa.

Date						
Time						
Lat						
Lon						
Description						
Measured depth						
Draft						
Sum 1						
Charted depth						
Tide height						
Sum 2						
Error						

References:

Inland & Coastal Navigation, 2nd Ed. Chapter 8

TC-2. Currents Underway

At any time in the passage, compare the speed over ground (SOG) with the knotmeter speed (S) and the course over ground (COG) with your present magnetic heading (H). That is Part A. Just make a few recordings of these measurements to become more aware of the differences.

Part B is at any later time, use the above information to compute the Set and Drift of the current which might account for the differences observed. Then Part C, look up the currents for the time and place of your observations to see how well they agree. Part B requires learning how to solve the vector triangle, or just cranking out the solution with a computer or phone app.

Part C requires learning how to interpolate and extrapolate the current tables, or, when using electronic charting, how to extrapolate the given data at nearby locations into the location of interest for the problem. You will usually not have to interpolate in this method since you can find the data for any specific time, whereas the tables only give the data for the peak and slack times.

Part A									
Date									
Time									
Lat									
Lon									
Description									
Knotmeter speed									
SOG									
Heading									
COG									
Part B									
Computed Set									
Computed Drift									
Part C									
Predicted Set									
Predicted Drift									

References:

Inland & Coastal Navigation, 2nd Ed. Chapter 8, Chapter 12, Section 12.19

Radar

R-1. Basic Radar Controls

Enter the times and dates that you have learned how to use the listed functions of the radar. Only make the entry after you feel confident that you know how these functions work. Note that some sound simple, but there may be nuances, so do not hesitate to ask about these if questions arise. Fill in other learned functions as they occur.

Function	Date	Time	Function	Date	Time	Function	Date	Time
On / Off / Warm-up			Plot / wake options					
Brilliance								
Gain								
Range								
Range Rings								
VRM								
EBL								

References:

Radar For Mariners, Revised Edition Chapters 1, 2

R-2. Confirm GPS Position Using Radar Range and Bearing

This is a standard procedure in navigation. From the GPS position either plotted on a chart or shown on an electronic chart, choose what might appear to be a conspicuous radar target and then determine from the chart what the range and bearing should be to that object. Then turn to the radar to confirm that this is right.

Date	Time	Lat/Lon	Description	Chart R and B	Radar R and B

References:

Radar For Mariners, Revised Edition Chapter 4

R-3. Distinguish Buoys and Moving Vessels

Buoys move straight down the radar screen with a speed of relative motion (SRM) equal to your own speed (S). Moving vessels can travel in any direction on the screen at various speeds. To prepare for more advanced analysis, start by identifying several buoys, anchored vessels, islets, etc that are not moving. Confirm identification by measuring their SRMs and compare with your knotmeter speed. Measurements will not often be exact, but should be close enough for identification.

Date	Time	Range	SRM	S	Date	Time	Range	SRM	S

References:

Radar For Mariners, Revised Edition Chapter 6

R-4. Closest Point of Approach

A key question to be answered by radar is how close will an approaching vessel pass us if we both remain on the same course and speed. This is best evaluated using the plot option on the radar, which can then be projected forward to estimate the CPA. Record several examples of your predicting the CPA and record at what range you made the observation.

Then use the SRM or other tricks to figure the time of the CPA (TCPA). If you ended up passing without course alterations (your's or their's)—in which case their trails will remain a straight line (ie more or less strait smear)—then record the actual time and CPA of the passing. If someone needed to alter course, then skip last two answers and mark through the spaces.

Date	Time	Range	CPA	TCPA	CPA real	TCPA real	Comments

References:

Radar For Mariners, Revised Edition Chapter 6

R-5. Relative Motion Diagram (Rapid Radar Plotting)

For any approaching (or diverging) target, figure its true course and speed by solving the relative motion diagram (RMD). You can take the data from the radar screen and then solve it on paper, or do the plotting right on the screen using a suitable marker.

This process will take some instruction from a text or instructor, but once understood, this most fundamental aspect of radar observing can be mastered with little practice. The Starpath Radar Trainer software is an excellent way to practice this, underway or at home. T1, R1, B1 = time, range and bearing of first observation, same with second, some 6 minutes or so later on.

Date	Course	Speed	T1	R1	B1	T2	R2	B2	SRM	DRM	TC	TS

References:

Radar For Mariners, Revised Edition Chapter 11

R-6. Radar Piloting

By this we mean the use of radar to aid your navigation without resorting to an actual Lat/Lon position fix. Methods include use of VRM as a danger circle or other form of guide, using SHL (ships heading line or heading marker) to align with a destination of choice, or that you are running parallel to shore, not getting set, etc. There are very many ways to improvise and any voyage will generate its own examples. In this exercise just record your time and location and make a text note of the tricks you used or were demonstrated. You will then have record of a real place that used the technique.

#	Date	Time	H	S	Lat/Lon	Description of location
1						
2						
3						
4						
5						
6						
7						
8						
9						
10						

#	Description of piloting method used in the situation listed above
1	
2	
3	
4	
5	
6	
7	
8	
9	
10	

References:

Radar For Mariners, Revised Edition Chapter 5

Inland & Coastal Navigation, 2nd Ed. Chapter 6, Section 6.12

R-7. Position Fix with Radar

Use some method of radar piloting to perform a fix underway or at anchor. Compare with the GPS result. Methods (Type) include Range and Bearing (RB), two or three ranges (xR), range and tangents (RT). Procedures are given in text or from instructor.

If you are moving rapidly, these will need to be running fixes for most precision, but that is fine point to be illustrated by an instructor. You can record the actual Lat/Lon for each or just the distance between the two fixes ("Error"). H = your heading, S = your speed.

Date	Time	H	S	Type	Radar Fix Lat/Lon	GPS Fix Lat/Lon	Error

References:

Radar For Mariners, Revised Edition Chapter 5

Inland & Coastal Navigation, 2nd Ed. Chapter 6, Section 6.12

Navigation Rules

NR-1. Reading Assignments

On board you will find a copy of the Navigation Rules, or there are many options to download a pdf or other app for your phone. It appears a long book and maybe complex when just skimming it. But with guidance, it is actually easy reading and quite interesting, and needless to say valuable. This is the most important book in all of navigation. The Rules will be discussed often in the pilothouse and throughout the voyage, so you might want to check out a copy and do some reading in short segments. Here is a suggested approach, with a form to fill in the date you completed the section. Each is actually very short.

   For now, read only the International Rules on the left-hand side of the page. Each assignment will take only about 15 minutes or so, with a bit more to think on it. Then bring your questions to an instructor or the skipper as they might arise. [We shall end up running the mile, by starting out walking a hundred yards at a time.]

Date	Assignment	Rules — Page count
	Part B, Sec I. Rules that apply all times, regardless of visibility	Rules 4 to 10 — 6 pages
	Part B, Sec II. Rules that apply when vessels can see each other	Rules 11 to 18 — 5 pages
	Part C, Lights and Shapes (power, fishing, and sailing)	Rules 23, 25, 26 — 12 pages
	Part C, Lights and Shapes (tow boat lights)	Rule 24 — 10 pages
	Part C, Lights and Shapes (anchored and aground)	Rule 30 — 3 pages
	Part D, Sound and Light Signals (maneuvering and warning)	Rule 34 — 2 pages
	Part D, Sound and Light Signals ("fog signals")	Rule 35 — 2 pages
	Part D, Sound and Light Signals (distress and getting attention)	Rules 37 and 36 — 2 pages

References:

Inland & Coastal Navigation, 2nd Ed. Chapter 10

NR-2. Sound Signals Underway

On any long voyage you are likely to hear some examples of the sound signals covered in the Rules. The frequency of hearing them, however, depends a lot on where you are. Mid-ocean you won't hear many. You will hear more on East Coast waters than on the West Coast waters (this should not be the case, but it is) and of course you hear more in confined waterways like the Intracoastal Waterway, sections of the Inside Passage to Alaska, and so forth, than you do in more open waters.

Sounds you will hear include maneuvering and "attention-getters" as well as danger and warning signals. Please note what you hear and when as well as what the signals mean. If you hear a light house fog signal record that as well and identify it... don't mix up a light house and a vessel, there is a famous joke in navigation about that.

Look up the definitions of the various signals and use the proper names, ie "prolonged" is not the same as "long." Time the signals if you can. See Rule 32 and Rule 36. You may also here gongs or bells, see Rule 30. If you hear a buoy, record that as well here. This is for all sounds related to navigation. There is also another more general section CW-4 on buoys.

Date	Time	Lat/Lon	Location description	Sound heard	Explanation

References:

Inland & Coastal Navigation, 2nd Ed. Chapter 10

NR-3. Lights Underway

How much you run at night will depend on the voyage and conditions underway. But even if you do not run much at night, you will likely be anchored or moored near open water where you might study lights from vessels underway or at anchor. Here is a place to record a few of the more prominent ones you see and identify. Record especially those that were difficult to identify because of extra lights showing, unusual aspect, etc.

The *aspect* of the vessel you are looking at is the relative bearing of your vessel from the other one, usually labeled port or starboard or red or green. If we are looking at the port bow of another vessel, its aspect would be 045 red. Your reference is the Nav Rules. This exercise is for vessel lights only; use CW-5 for recording and identifying navigation lights such as on buoys or lighthouses.

Date	Time	Lat/Lon	Location description	Vessel lights	ID = vessel type / aspect

References:

Inland & Coastal Navigation, 2nd Ed. Chapter 10

NR-4. Right of Way

We learn the rules by first studying, then doing. At each encounter you will ask yourself about right of way. Usually the answer will be clear from the studying, but there inevitably will be times when questions arise. These are the events to record here.

Cases you ran across that taught you something or presented some special issue. Suppose two boats are approaching you from different directions, or you see at night what appears to be a monstrous Christmas tree coming down the channel (a common disguise of cruise ships), etc.

Don't hesitate to ask the skipper or an instructor about what you see on the water, even when you are not on watch. When on watch it is of course crucial to ask, if there are any doubts at all about a traffic encounter.

Date	Time	Lat/Lon	Location description	Situation

References:

Inland & Coastal Navigation, 2nd Ed. Chapter 10

NR-5. Rule 19d

This is a rule that has most to do with radar in the fog. From Section II of Part B you learned that when two vessels approach each other with risk of collision, one has "right of way" over the other—in all cases but one (what is the exception?). But Section II assumes the vessels can see each other. If you know from radar alone in the fog that risk of collision is developing, then Section II Rules do not apply (although Section I Rules do still apply.)

In short, *there is no right of way in the fog*, so we must rely on special rules to tell us what to do in this case. This is Rule 19d. Hence, read Rule 19 (Section III), it is one page long, and think on it so you can answer the questionnaire on radar maneuvering in the fog.

Date	Assignment	Rules — Page count
	Part B, Sec III. Rules that apply when you cannot see each other	Rule 19 — 1 page

A reminder on relative bearings: dead ahead = 000 R, starboard beam = 090 R, port beam = 270 R, etc. With that in mind, study wording of Rule 19 to answer what your maneuver should be when you detect by radar a vessel approaching from the directions given in the questionnaire below, but you cannot see them visually. Assume you watched each approach from more than 8 mi off and it is now say 5 miles off but definitely headed toward you.

Answer which way you should turn, if any, and when, or should you change speed? etc. AND PLEASE REMEMBER, these are only exercises intended to get you thinking about this Rule. Every situation will be different in reality and there is no one right answer that unambiguously applies in all cases. One of the main rules of the Rules is Rule 2b (please read it) that states you may have to depart from the Rules to avoid a collision, and indeed should do so if need be.

After filling in your maneuver, list the Rules that guide your answer, ie 19d(i) , 8a, etc. [This Rule is discussed in great detail in the Starpath Radar Trainer 3, including animations to illustrate the maneuvers.]

Date	Approach from	Your maneuver assuming target vessel is not in sight visually	Rules reference
	000 R		
	045 R		
	090 R		
	135 R		
	180 R		
	225 R		
	270 R		
	315 R		

References:

Inland & Coastal Navigation, 2nd Ed. Chapter 10

Radar For Mariners, Revised Edition Chapter 12

Piloting

P-1. Bearing Fix

Use a hand bearing compass to find your position from crossed bearings. Record the time of each sight and your GPS position at the time of the first sight. Use two or three objects for each fix. Record course (C) and speed (S) so we can correct these for motion later if need be. Plot the fix on paper chart or electronic and then figure the Range and Bearing from the your plotted fix to your actual position, ie the error in your fix. Also record an estimate (ie 0.2 nmi) of the uncertainty in your fix (delta).

#	Date	Time	Bearing	Target	C	S	Lat/Lon from GPS		
1									
2							Range	Bearing	delta
3									

#	Date	Time	Bearing	Target	C	S	Lat/Lon from GPS		
1									
2							Range	Bearing	delta
3									

#	Date	Time	Bearing	Target	C	S	Lat/Lon from GPS		
1									
2							Range	Bearing	delta
3									

#	Date	Time	Bearing	Target	C	S	Lat/Lon from GPS		
1									
2							Range	Bearing	delta
3									

#	Date	Time	Bearing	Target	C	S	Lat/Lon from GPS		
1									
2							Range	Bearing	delta
3									

References:

Inland & Coastal Navigation, 2nd Ed. Chapter 6, Section 6.3

P-2. LOP by Natural Ranges

Often the most accurate piloting fix comes from ranges. When available, establish a Line of Position and document it here. First identify a range that you are on or anticipate crossing. Then note the time you cross it visually. Draw this range on a chart (paper or electronic) and compare to your actual GPS position at the time. Also record "delta," precise difference from your position and nearest position on the range. Note that delta can be very small for this type of observation if done carefully.

Date	Time	GPS Lat/Lon	Range description	delta

References:

Inland & Coastal Navigation, 2nd Ed. Chapter 6, Section 6.2

P-3. Fix by Soundings

In some cases, a single bearing or range line combined with a sounding will give a fix, or in special cases, soundings alone might give at least an approximate fix. If conditions are right, try one of these. Note when tides are large, the depth must be corrected for the tide, although in some cases the measurements are not very sensitive to tide height as in going on and off a prominent shelf.

This item P-3 is just a place to record your measurement results. You will need to keep the details in your own notebook. One method might be do note an underwater shelf you are traveling across, then note the time, log, and course when you enter the shelf and again when you exit, and from that data you can figure out where you are. Demonstration from an instructor will be helpful for the fist couple.

Date	Time	GPS Lat/Lon	Method tried	delta

References:

Inland & Coastal Navigation, 2nd Ed. Chapter 6, Section 6.4

P-4. COP from Vertical Sextant Angle

Identify a landmark in sight whose elevation (H) you can determine from a chart. Use a sextant to measure the vertical angle from top of landmark (whose elevation you know) to the waterline below it. Record sextant angle (Hs) and bearing to the object. Use formula, tables, or calculator (StarPilot) to determine distance off (D) based on H and Hs.

From this, draw a Circle of Position on the chart centered on the landmark with radius equal to D to see how close your GPS position is to this circle (delta). [Note there are actually three techniques that can be applied using vertical sextant angles to find distance off depending on how far off you are. See text or an instructor for details.]

Date	Time	GPS Lat/Lon	Target name	H	Hs	D	delta

References:

Inland & Coastal Navigation, 2nd Ed. Chapter 6, Section 6.10

How to Use Plastic Sextants Part 3

P-5. Three-body Fix by Sextant

This technique, though little used these days, remains the most accurate means of piloting underway, and it can even be one of the quickest methods when using a three-arm protractor. It can also be carried out quite nicely with an inexpensive plastic sextant such as the Davis Mark 3.

Use the sextant horizontally to measure the angles between 3 bodies A, B, and C, where each is separated by some 20 to 80° apart (angle A to B and angle B to C). They can be in any direction, three in a row on the horizon works well. You will also learn that some combinations will not work (when you and the 3 bodies all lie on or near the same circle there is no solution).

The easiest solution is to use a 3-arm protractor and a paper chart, but we can also do this by obtaining the Lat/Lon of the targets from an electronic chart and then solving for the fix mathematically. After you get your fix compare to the GPS fix. The difference is delta. Also record your solution method which would be 3-arm, computed, or plotted. This exercise is best done after some instruction, then it is easy.

Date	Time	GPS Lat/Lon	A to B	B to C	Solution method	delta

References:

Inland & Coastal Navigation, 2nd Ed. Chapter 6, Section 6.13

How to Use Plastic Sextants Part 3

Electronic Charting

EC-1. Basic Skills

Confirm when you have learned these skills with the charting program. Note that some crew members may have learned some ahead of you, so you can learn from one another as well as from the instructor. Once you feel you have mastered the skill, log the time and date. Add to the list as you learn new operations. Keep details of the instructions in your own notebook.

Operation	Date	Time	Operation	Date	Time
Select charts and load chart of choice			R and B boat to point		
Scroll, center, zoom			R and B point to point		
Set scales, windows			Use of Cross Track Error XTE		
Read Lat/Lon of boat position			Use of Tides and Currents		
Set marks, properties, hide/show					
Set up a route, activate a waypoint					
Use of Plan Book					
Monitor GPS input signals					
Display multiple windows					
Split and join routes					
Set up projected boat position					
Use of range rings					

References:

Inland & Coastal Navigation, 2nd Ed. Chapter 7

EC-2. Route Monitoring Underway

Once underway to an active waypoint on a leg of a route, confirm that you have made these observations as a means of practice with electronic charting. Record your present position, the name or number of next waypoint (WP), range to WP (R), bearing to WP (B), ship's heading (H), plus course over ground (COG), speed over ground, cross track error (XTE), velocity made good (VMG), and the estimated time of arrival (ETA).

If it works out, also record the actual time of arrival at that WP (TA). [You may not have the heading from the station you are working from unless all nav stations onboard are sharing the same NMEA stream of data or you have a compass near by, but all the rest of this can be obtained from a deck chair and handheld GPS. That is, this is identical to GPS-2 in Section 8, but now being worked rather easier using e-charts.]

Date	Time	Next WP	R	B	H	COG	SOG	XTE	VMG	ETA	TA

References:

Inland & Coastal Navigation, 2nd Ed. Chapter 7

GPS Navigation

GPS-1. Basic Skills

Record the time and date that you have learned these skills either with your own hand held unit or with the ship's GPS. Fill in new skills as learned.

Operation	Date	Time	Operation	Date	Time
Read and interpret Lat and Lon					
Entering a waypoint					
Entering a route					
Read R and B to waypoint					
Reading COG and SOG					
Read and understand XTE					
Display, zoom, and pan the plot screen					
Advance to next waypoint on a route					
Arrival alarms					
Interpret active satellite data					

References:

Inland & Coastal Navigation, 2nd Ed. Chapter 7

GPS-2. Route Monitoring Underway

This is the same exercise we have in the electronic charting section, but this time it is done all with the GPS, either mounted or handheld, without reference to any chart, electronic or paper. Once underway to an active waypoint on a leg of a route, confirm that you have made these observations as a means of practice with electronic charting.

Record your present position, the name or number of next waypoint (WP), range to WP (R), bearing to WP (B), ship's heading (H), plus course over ground (COG), speed over ground, cross track error (XTE), velocity made good (VMG), and the estimated time of arrival (ETA). If it works out, also record the actual time of arrival at that WP (TA).

Date	Time	Next WP	R	B	H	COG	SOG	XTE	VMG	ETA	TA

References:

Inland & Coastal Navigation, 2nd Ed. Chapter 7

GPS-3. Confirm Position Accuracy

From a stationary position at anchor or dock, record the GPS position, having it watched it carefully to be sure you have evaluated and averaged the "jitter," ie in latitude 47° 34.567 note if it is really a 7 or 6 or 8 that should be the last digit, and what is the average amount it is bouncing around.

Record Latitude jitter as, ie 0.003, meaning this last decimal is bouncing around about that much. Also note that the GPS is set to the same datum as the chart is (WSG84, NAD 27, etc). Note you may have to compute delta since it will be small.

Time	Date	GPS Lat/Lon	Lat jitter	Chart Lat/Lon	delta

References:

Inland & Coastal Navigation, 2nd Ed. Chapter 7

Dead Reckoning

DR-1. Basic Terms

Make a record that the following terms have been explained and are understood, by noting here the actual times that you first used these yourself during some navigation process. It is fundamental that these terms be understood completely.

Term	Time	Date	Term	Time	Date
Heading (H)			Knotmeter speed (S)		
Course (C)			Speed over ground (SOG)		
Course over ground			Velocity made good (VMG)		
Bearing to WP			Speed of Advance (SOA)		

References:

Inland & Coastal Navigation, 2nd Ed. Chapter 5, Section 5.1

DR-2. ETA to Waypoint

Basic speed-time-distance problems occur continuously in navigation. Here we practice one part of the problem. Check with instructor for various tricks, calculator short cuts, etc. We combine this exercise with more practice on reading distances from a chart, paper or electronic, and later add to it corrections for current as they might apply.

Identify several consecutive waypoints of the day's run and figure the distance from the Start WP to the End WP you have selected (called D). Have it be at least a 3-hour run, starting from a waypoint we have recently passed with logged time of passing (Start Time). Then use whatever speeds you need from present data to predict the time we will arrive at the End way point (ETA at End).

Then when we do pass the End WP (assuming we have not had to alter course or plans significantly) record the actual time of arrival (TA at end) there and compare with your prediction (delta T). You can use a name or number to identify the waypoints. For now we are not doing current corrections directly, but you can take this into account by choosing SOG, for example, instead of just S.

Date	Start WP	Start Time	End WP	Dis-tance	ETA at End	TA at End	delta T

References:

Inland & Coastal Navigation, 2nd Ed. Chapter 5, Section 5.4

DR-3. Magnetic Variation

On many long voyages (and even some short ones in some parts of the world) the magnetic variation will change. We are usually aware of this from chart plotting, but it does not hurt to make record of this independently. Also on such voyages, check that the GPS and e-chart software are not locked into some "manual" variation mode which lets you enter it, but then will not let it change automatically as needed.

Generally speaking, the electronic auto variation functions in GPS units work well, and in principle they could be more accurate than the charts since they give it to you by Lat/Lon according to the present date. We will also use this exercise to compare a charted variation value (which may need corrected for date, depending on how old the chart is) and a value from a GPS unit.

To get the chart value, look for a compass rose printed on the chart nearest your Lat/Lon position. The date correction is also on that rose. You might look ahead to the value at your destination to see how many points you might be entering. At Port Townsend WA, for example, the variation is 19.1° E and at Petersburg, AK it is 24.0° E, so on this voyage 4 or 5 entries would give you notice of every 1° change.

Date	Lat/Lon	Location Description	Charted var	GPS var

References:

Inland & Coastal Navigation, 2nd Ed. Chapter 4, Sections 4.2, 4.6

DR-4. Compass Check on Range

When the boat is sailing a well defined range which you can identify on the chart, you have a golden opportunity for a quick check of the compass. Just look up the magnetic heading of the range and compare it with the compass heading while you are on that range.

The difference is your deviation (Dev) on that particular heading. It is standard procedure to make this check whenever the opportunity presents itself. It is best done with *navigational ranges* that are set up and charted for entering channels or harbors, etc.

You might also do it with a *natural range* which is just any two items that you can identify on the chart and get an accurate range from that is in line with your heading. Buoys, however, should not be a component of the range since they can move. It must be made from solid landmarks of some sort.

Date	Time	Lat/Lon	Range Description	Chart H	Compass H	Dev

References:

Inland & Coastal Navigation, 2nd Ed. Chapter 4, Sections 4.5

Weather

W-1. VHF Weather Sources

On VHF radio, scroll through the weather channels and record which stations are available. A personal portable VHF would be nice for this. Record the VHF channel, the station call sign and location if given. Listen to the full broadcast and make notes of subject given, ie reports R, synopsis S, forecast F, and also record the regions covered. You may hear broadcasts that are not where you are. Some may be helpful, if you are eventually going there, others might not be.

The form below includes possibility of hearing up to 4 stations at the same time and location, but it will be more likely to hear just 1 or 2, sometimes 3. Try to do it once a day if possible. Note this exercise is not for the content, just sources. W-2 will work with the content. Remember there are Coast Guard as well as Weather Service broadcasts in some cases.

Time	Date	Lat/Lon	Description
VHF Chan	**Call sign or station ID**	**Subjects**	

Time	Date	Lat/Lon	Description
VHF Chan	**Call sign or station ID**	**Subjects**	

Time	Date	Lat/Lon	Description
VHF Chan	**Call sign or station ID**	**Subjects**	

Time	Date	Lat/Lon	Description

VHF Chan	Call sign or station ID	Subjects	

Time	Date	Lat/Lon	Description

VHF Chan	Call sign or station ID	Subjects	

Time	Date	Lat/Lon	Description

VHF Chan	Call sign or station ID	Subjects	

Time	Date	Lat/Lon	Description

VHF Chan	Call sign or station ID	Subjects	

References:

Modern Marine Weather, 2nd Ed. Chapter 8

W-2. VHF Weather Reports

Find the best channel for your present location. Listen to the full report and record wind, seas, and weather at nearest reporting station (you will need to refer to the chart or marine weather services guide). Then record your present conditions. Then note the forecast for where you go next. This exercise may take some time if you are not familiar with the regions covered, but it is a crucial exercise for any voyage.

If you don't have access to instruments onboard, then just estimate the wind speed and direction and the sea state. "Weather" = fog, rain, sunny, etc. You may need to record this data on scratch paper and then transcribe to here if there are many reports and you do not know ahead of time which ones will be pertinent.

Time	Date	Lat/Lon	Description

Nearest report locations	Time	Wind, seas, weather, barometer

Your own observations =		
Nearest forecast locations		Wind, seas, weather

Time	Date	Lat/Lon	Description

Nearest report locations	Time	Wind, seas, weather, barometer

Your own observations =		
Nearest forecast locations		Wind, seas, weather

Time	Date		Lat/Lon	Description

Nearest report locations		Time	Wind, seas, weather, barometer

Your own observations =			
Nearest forecast locations			Wind, seas, weather

Time	Date		Lat/Lon	Description

Nearest report locations		Time	Wind, seas, weather, barometer

Your own observations =			
Nearest forecast locations			Wind, seas, weather

Time	Date		Lat/Lon	Description

Nearest report locations		Time	Wind, seas, weather, barometer

Your own observations =			
Nearest forecast locations			Wind, seas, weather

Time	Date	Lat/Lon	Description

Nearest report locations	Time	Wind, seas, weather, barometer

Your own observations =		

Nearest forecast locations		Wind, seas, weather

Time	Date	Lat/Lon	Description

Nearest report locations	Time	Wind, seas, weather, barometer

Your own observations =		

Nearest forecast locations		Wind, seas, weather

Time	Date	Lat/Lon	Description

Nearest report locations	Time	Wind, seas, weather, barometer

Your own observations =		

Nearest forecast locations		Wind, seas, weather

References:

Modern Marine Weather, 2nd Ed. Chapter 8

W-3. Cloud Spotting

From the list below, mark the times you spotted the particular formations. Remember, there can be many types in the sky at any one time, and that the type of a given cloud mass can evolve from one form to another over relatively short periods of time. Entries do not have to be at the same time. Just when you see one, enter in any empty slot.

Type	Date	Time	Date	Time	Date	Time	Date	Time	Date	Time
Cumulus										
Cumulonimbus										
Stratus										
Nimbostratus										
Altostratus										
Altocumulus										
Stratocumulus										
Cirrostratus										
Cirrocumulus										
Cirrus										

References:

Modern Marine Weather, 2nd Ed.
Chapter 5

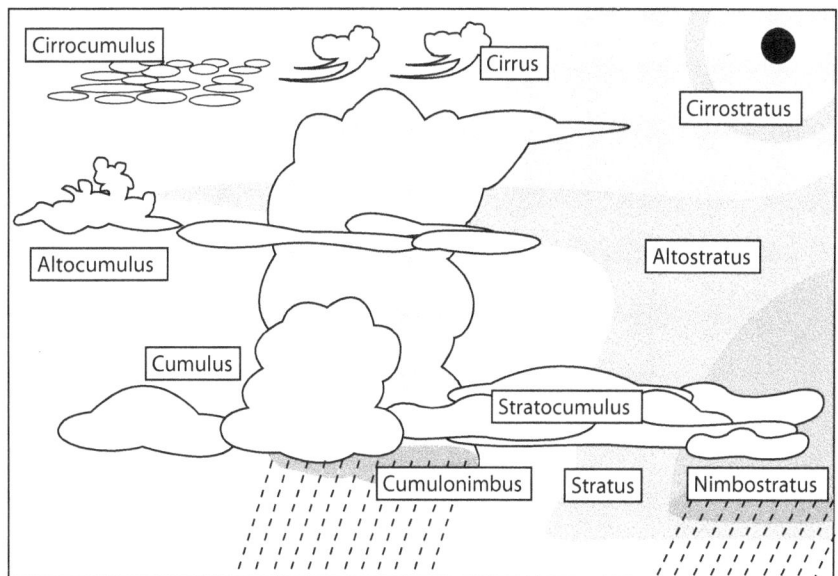

W-4. Apparent Wind to True Wind

Record apparent wind speed and angle along with course and speed and from these solve for true wind speed (TWS) and true wind angle (TWA). Then compute true wind direction (TWD) = course ± TWA. Do your work in your nav notebook and just record the results here.

Note that all measurements will require some averaging. None of these values are steady. You can solve for true wind by plotting out the vectors or using a computer or calculator. There are apps that do this job nicely, as will a computer in the Starpath Weather Trainer.

Date	Time	AWA	AWS	Course	Speed	TWS	TWA	TWD

References:

Modern Marine Weather, 2nd Ed. Chapter 2, Section 2.5

W-5. Barometer Comparisons

Z = zulu = nickname for GMT = Universal Time = official time system for navigation and weather. Record our barometer at a synoptic time (00Z, 06Z, 12Z, or 18Z = 1700, 2300, 0500, 1100 PDT = 5 and 11 AM and PM, PDT) as well as our GPS position at that time. Then compare that with the pressure you interpolate from the corresponding surface analysis map.

Try to download these maps and keep them posted or in the computer. The key here is getting your own baro at the right time or noting that it has not changed, or noting that it is easy to interpolate from what you have recorded. If you need it at 1100 and you have it at 10 and again at 12, then the 1100 value is likely in between the two.

Time	Date	Lat/Lon	Ship's baro	Interpolated map baro

References:

Modern Marine Weather, 2nd Ed. Chapter 2, Section 2.2

The Barometer Handbook Chapter 6, Section 6.3

Celestial Navigation

CN-1. Star Spotting

"Navigational stars" are the 57 listed on the Daily Pages of the *Nautical Almanac.* They are the same throughout the year, although only some 20 or so might be visible during the night from any given location and date—others are below the horizon all night. From the *Nautical Almanac* star maps or from a 2102-D Star Finder, identify as many navigation stars as you can and make note of when you observed them.

Various phone apps are especially valuable for this. Remember, though, that this is definitely a peripheral exercise in that one does not need to know anything at all about the stars or how to find them in order to do successful celestial navigation.

We only train navigators to find the stars because other crew members are going to assume we know how to do this! Enter an estimate of the height (ie Hs = 35°) and true bearing (Zn = 075) of the star as well. Crew member with largest count gets a prize.

Date	Time	Lat/Lon	Star Name	Hs	Zn

References:

Celestial Navigation, 2nd Ed. Chapter 10

CN-2. Twilight Times

On any clear afternoon, look up the time of sunset from the *Nautical Almanac* (NA). This will require a correction for Lon. Then look up the time of Civil Twilight and Nautical Twilight from the NA. Then watch the sky clearly after sunset to note when you see the first star (or planet). Note its approximate height (Hs) and true bearing (Zn).

Record this time and data. This will be at about the time of Civil Twilight that you recorded—or just make the observations and then later come back and look up the times. The latter can be done any time. To expand the exercise, figure out what the body was that you first observed. Note that in some parts of the world it is not always clear enough to do this exercise, so SEIZE THE MOMENT when available.

Date	Lat/Lon	Sunset	Civil Twi	Naut Twi	Sight time	Hs	Zn	Body

References:

Celestial Navigation, 2nd Ed. Chapter 5, Section 5.2

CN-3. Checking Watch Time

As a rule, any GPS unit in contact with satellites will have the time correct to the second. So you can use the GPS to set your watch, or you can also use the WWV broadcast on a SW radio. Record method here as GPS or WWV and try each at some point. After setting your watch at the first entry, make another entry every day or so to record your watch error, but *do not set it again.* We want to observe the watch error increasing over the period of the voyage. Record the date and time you checked it and the erorr. With practice you might estimate the error to within 0.5 seconds.

Date	Time	WE (F or S)	Date	Time	WE (F or S)	Date	Time	WE (F or S)
		Set to 0.0						

Then plot the Watch Error vs Date to figure the Rate of the watch (seconds gained or loss per day or per 3 days etc). You can read this from the slope of the plot. Doesn't matter if gaining or losing, it will increase. Try to plot proportional to the value in the spaces provided, ie 6.0 s in the middle, 6.5 s on the line, etc. Same with dates, the width of a horizontal space is 24 hr, so noon is in the middle, etc. Note all dates go in consecutively, even if you do not have data on that date.

WE
12s
11s
10s
9s
8s
7s
6s
5s
4s
3s
2s
1s
Date =

CN-4. Compass Checks from the Sun

With celestial navigation it is a simple matter to compute the true direction to the sun at any moment and from that what it should read on a compass. All you need is your position and the time and the local magnetic variation (Var). If you have a way to correlate that direction (or a shadow's direction) to the centerline of the vessel, you have a convenient and potentially accurate way to check the ship's compass.

Record here any opportunities you might have to do this yourself or see it demonstrated. Once seen, it is easy to do on your own. Even if you do not know celestial, you can learn how to get the sun's bearing from various apps or www.starpath.com/usno, which involves just pushing a few buttons. Again, you will have more details in your notebook and just record the events here. Compass deviation depends on your heading, so any such measurement just applies to the heading you were on when you did the measurement. We do compass check with ranges in section DR-4. See references for compass conversions and this process in general.

Date	Time	GPS Lat/Lon	Var.	Heading	Sun Zn (M)	Sun Zn (C)	Deviation

CN-3 References:

Celestial Navigation, 2nd Ed. Chapter 1, Chapter 11, Section 11.2

CN-4 References:

Celestial Navigation, 2nd Ed. Chapter 11, Section 11.3

CN-5. Sun line Running Fix

If you have opportunity for cel nav underway, here is a place to record the sights taken and the results. Details must be kept in your own notebook, just put time and results here, along with delta the difference between cel nav and GPS fixes.

Date	Time	No of sights	Celestial Fix	GPS position	delta

References:

Celestial Navigation, 2nd Ed. Chapters 5 and 6

CN-6. Sun-Moon Fix

For a week or two each month the moon is in position for a daytime fix with the sun. If you get the chance, record results here. Planning moon sights with the sun is discussed with convenient tables in *The Star Finder Book*. Generally the best time is mid-morning or mid-afternoon with a half moon.

Date	Time	No of sights	Celestial Fix	GPS position	delta

References:

Celestial Navigation, 2nd Ed. Chapter 9

The Star Finder Book Chapter 3, Section 3.4, Table 3-3, Chapter 6

CN-7. Star-Planet Fix

If twilight sights are possible either underway or from an anchorage with good view to the horizon, the record them here. You might also plan the sights even if you do not get a chance to take them. Planning star-planet sights is a key process in celestial navigation. Review references below to figure the best sight combinations for any sky.

Date	Time	No of sights	Celestial Fix	GPS position	delta

References:

Celestial Navigation, 2nd Ed. Chapters 8 and 10

The Star Finder Book Chapter 6

Navigation Challenges

NC-1. Unforeseen Eventualities

All voyages involve both routine navigation planning and some special circumstances that take special care or a change in plans underway. Depending on the location, the special challenges might involve weather, traffic, currents, or maybe political issues like customs and clearance—if customs closes at 5 on Friday, hypothetically, and you get stuck in currents twice as strong as expected or head winds, etc., and you get there at 6, then you have faced a challenge.

Or your nav lights burned out and you did not have back up set, etc... buoys were missing, or off station, etc. Some piece of equipment failed, etc. Some can be anticipated, others will not be anticipated. But the special challenges will be clear by the time you get there. If there are none, then all the better. Give yourself an A+ for planning, otherwise, record them here for the record.

There is no right entry here. What is a challenge for some might be already second nature to others, who have been through that before, etc. Just record the events you want to remember. Restrict this list to matters other than issues with the Nav rules directly. You have a special section (NR-4) for recording those. Naturally, you may have more details about the events in your notebook, but this is just a log of the incidents.

Date	Time	GPS Lat/Lon	Special situation and solution

Starpath Reference List

Inland & Coastal Navigation, Second Edition by David Burch, Starpath Publications ISBN 978-0-914025-40-5

Radar For Mariners, Revised Edition by David Burch, McGraw-Hill ISBN 978-0-07-183039-3

How to Use Plastic Sextants by David Burch, Starpath Publications ISBN 978-0-914025-24-5

Modern Marine Weather, 2nd Ed., Second Edition by David Burch, Starpath Publications ISBN 978-0-914025-33-7

The Barometer Handbook by David Burch, Starpath Publications ISBN 978-0-914025-12-2

Celestial Navigation, 2nd Ed. , Second Edition by David Burch, Starpath Publications ISBN 978-0-914025-46-7

The Star Finder Book by David Burch, Starpath Publications ISBN 978-0-914025-00-9

Navigation Workbook 18465 Tr by David Burch and Larry Brandt, Starpath Publications ISBN 978-0-914025-45-0

Navigation Workbook 1210 Tr by David Burch and Larry Brandt, Starpath Publications ISBN 978-0-914025-44-3

Emergency Navigation, Second Edition by David Burch, McGraw-Hill ISBN 978-0-071481-84-7

General References

USCG Navigation Rules Handbook, available as printed book and ebooks

NavRules, an iOS app from Mintata Research

Starpath Nav Rules Trainer, software for PC

American Practical Navigator Pub. No. 9, NGA

Starpath Radar Trainer Software, PC radar simulator

Starpath Chart Trainer Software, an interactive, illustrated and annotated electronic version of Chart No. 1.

Standard References for any Voyage
all are available as pdf downloads , as well as print

NOAA Tide Tables

NOAA Current Tables

US Coast Pilot

USCG Light List

Navigation Rules Handbook

Chart No. 1

Personal Logbook

The following pages make up a personal logbook. This is intended for your own records and for getting into the process of record keeping. Your records here will also serve as an anchor reference for your own notebook or journal of the voyage. On watch you can use the ship's log and that is different from this. You can fill out your personal logbook at any time during the day.

We recommend noting departure and arrival plus three entries during the day. Just use whatever time is convenient that roughly matches the categories (mid morning, etc). It would also be best, if it works out, to choose a time when passing some prominent or otherwise descriptive point. On longer open passages, this will not be possible, but for most others it will be. Later at home you could, if you like, recreate our route in your own electronic chart program or plot it on charts.

You might also correlate some of the entries with other exercises you do in this book.

Here are the entries and how to fill them.

Day# starts from 1 and applies to all entries till next day. This category is just for a quick orientation in the log.

Date is your watch date in your local time zone, ie Pacific Daylight Time (PDT).

Time is local time, ie PDT in 24 hr system, ie 1300 = 1 pm.

Log is an accumulative odometer. There may be one in the pilothouse or nav station; they are also found in electronic charting programs. If you don't have this it is OK, the time and position will suffice.

Lat-Lon from the GPS or from the chart.

Course should be the magnetic compass course we are steering from the pilothouse or cockpit, or use COG from nearest GPS unit if that is more convenientand then mark it COG. (COG = course over ground.) Note this is our desired course; at any one moment the Heading might be off course a bit.

Speed is knotmeter speed which must be read from the pilothouse or nav station. If that is not convenient, just use SOG from nearest GPS unit and mark it as such. (SOG = speed over ground.)

Baro is the barometric pressure from the nearest barometer. Record in mb or tenths of mb if available, ie 1013.4 and mark the trend in some consistent manner for steady, rising, or falling.

AWS is apparent wind speed. This will be read from wind instruments in the nav station. One of the exercises will be to convert Apparent Wind to True Wind using Course and Speed.

AWA is the apparent wind angle. This is the angle off the bow that the apparent wind comes from. You can use 45P to mean 45° on the port bow, or use relative angles such as 315 R.

Location description and comments is where to add a brief text description of the place. This entry is important, don't just put in a Lat-Lon but include this as well. It is good practice in navigation to keep in mind the actual names of the places you pass.

	Day #	Date	Description	Time	Log	Lat/Lon	Course	Speed	Baro
1			Depart						
2			Mid-morning						
3			Mid-day						
4			Mid-afternoon						
5			Anchorage						
6			Depart						
7			Mid-morning						
8			Mid-day						
9			Mid-afternoon						
10			Anchorage						
11			Depart						
12			Mid-morning						
13			Mid-day						
14			Mid-afternoon						
15			Anchorage						
16			Depart						
17			Mid-morning						
18			Mid-day						
19			Mid-afternoon						
20			Anchorage						
21			Depart						
22			Mid-morning						
23			Mid-day						
24			Mid-afternoon						
25			Anchorage						
26			Depart						
27			Mid-morning						
28			Mid-day						
29			Mid-afternoon						
30			Anchorage						
	1	2	3	4	5	6	7	8	9

	AWS	AWA	Location Description and Comments
1			
2			
3			
4			
5			
6			
7			
8			
9			
10			
11			
12			
13			
14			
15			
16			
17			
18			
19			
20			
21			
22			
23			
24			
25			
26			
27			
28			
29			
30			
	10	11	12

	Day #	Date	Description	Time	Log	Lat/Lon	Course	Speed	Baro
1			Depart						
2			Mid-morning						
3			Mid-day						
4			Mid-afternoon						
5			Anchorage						
6			Depart						
7			Mid-morning						
8			Mid-day						
9			Mid-afternoon						
10			Anchorage						
11			Depart						
12			Mid-morning						
13			Mid-day						
14			Mid-afternoon						
15			Anchorage						
16			Depart						
17			Mid-morning						
18			Mid-day						
19			Mid-afternoon						
20			Anchorage						
21			Depart						
22			Mid-morning						
23			Mid-day						
24			Mid-afternoon						
25			Anchorage						
26			Depart						
27			Mid-morning						
28			Mid-day						
29			Mid-afternoon						
30			Anchorage						
	1	2	3	4	5	6	7	8	9

	AWS	AWA	Location Description and Comments
1			
2			
3			
4			
5			
6			
7			
8			
9			
10			
11			
12			
13			
14			
15			
16			
17			
18			
19			
20			
21			
22			
23			
24			
25			
26			
27			
28			
29			
30			
	10	11	12

Plotting Sheets

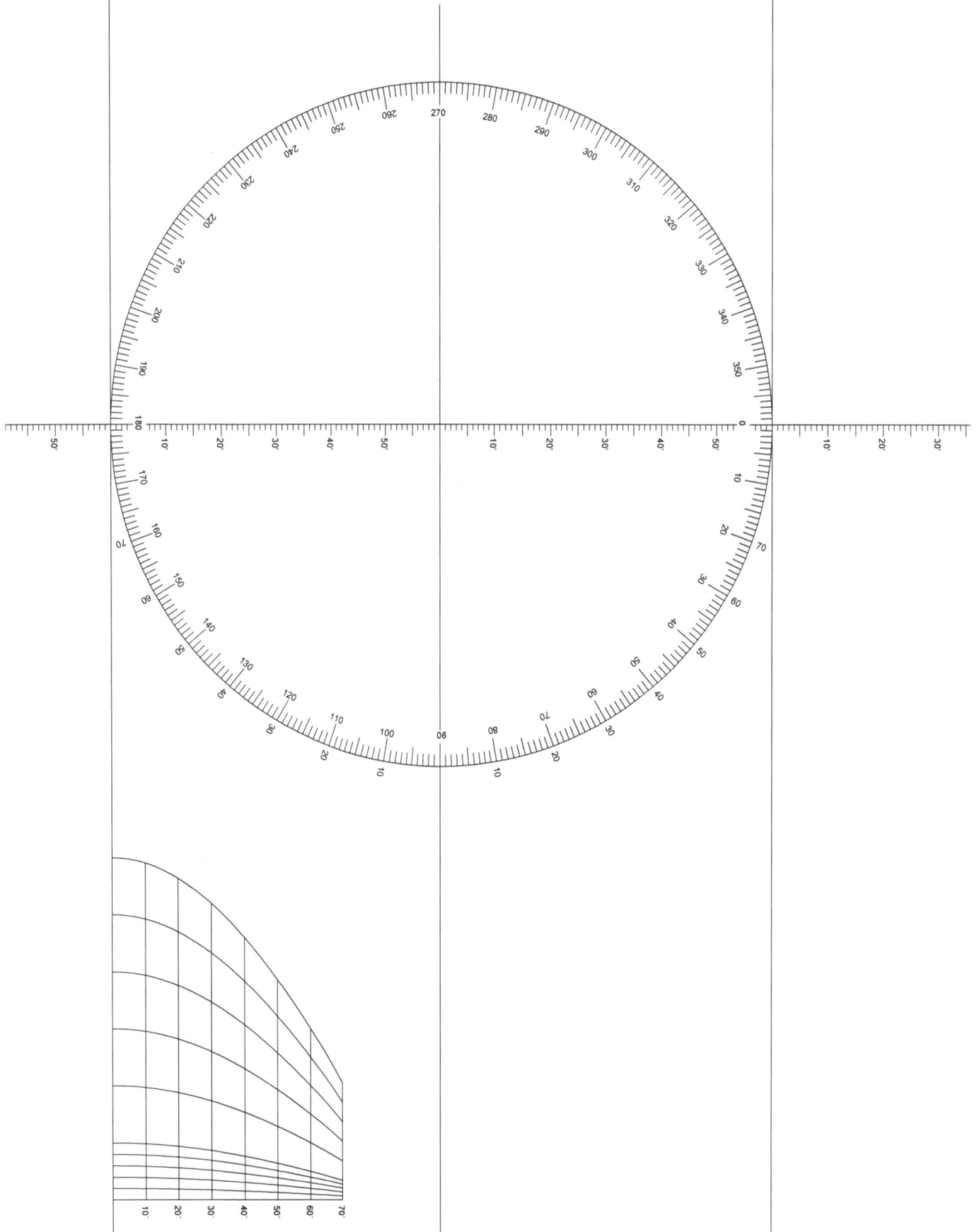

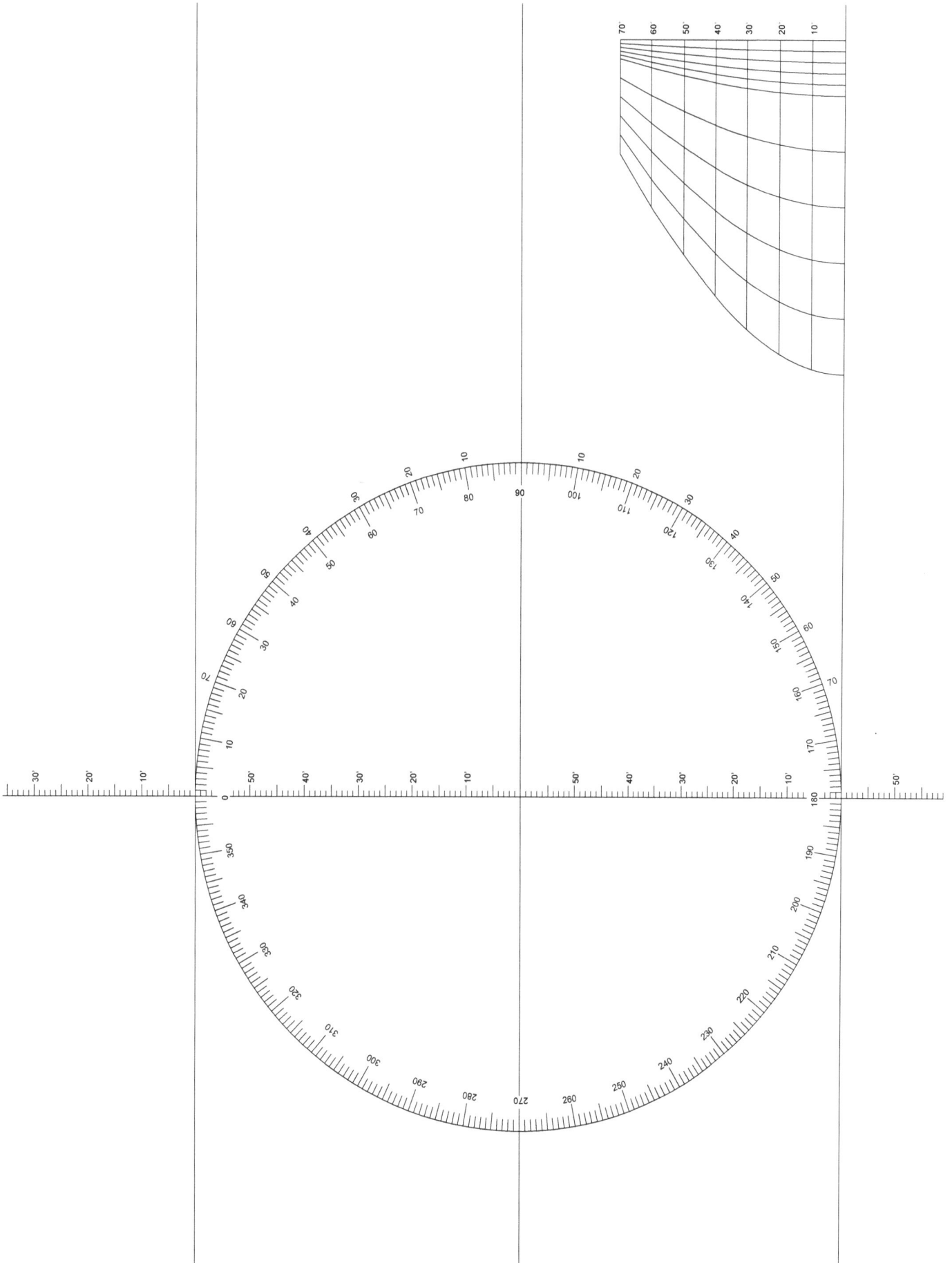

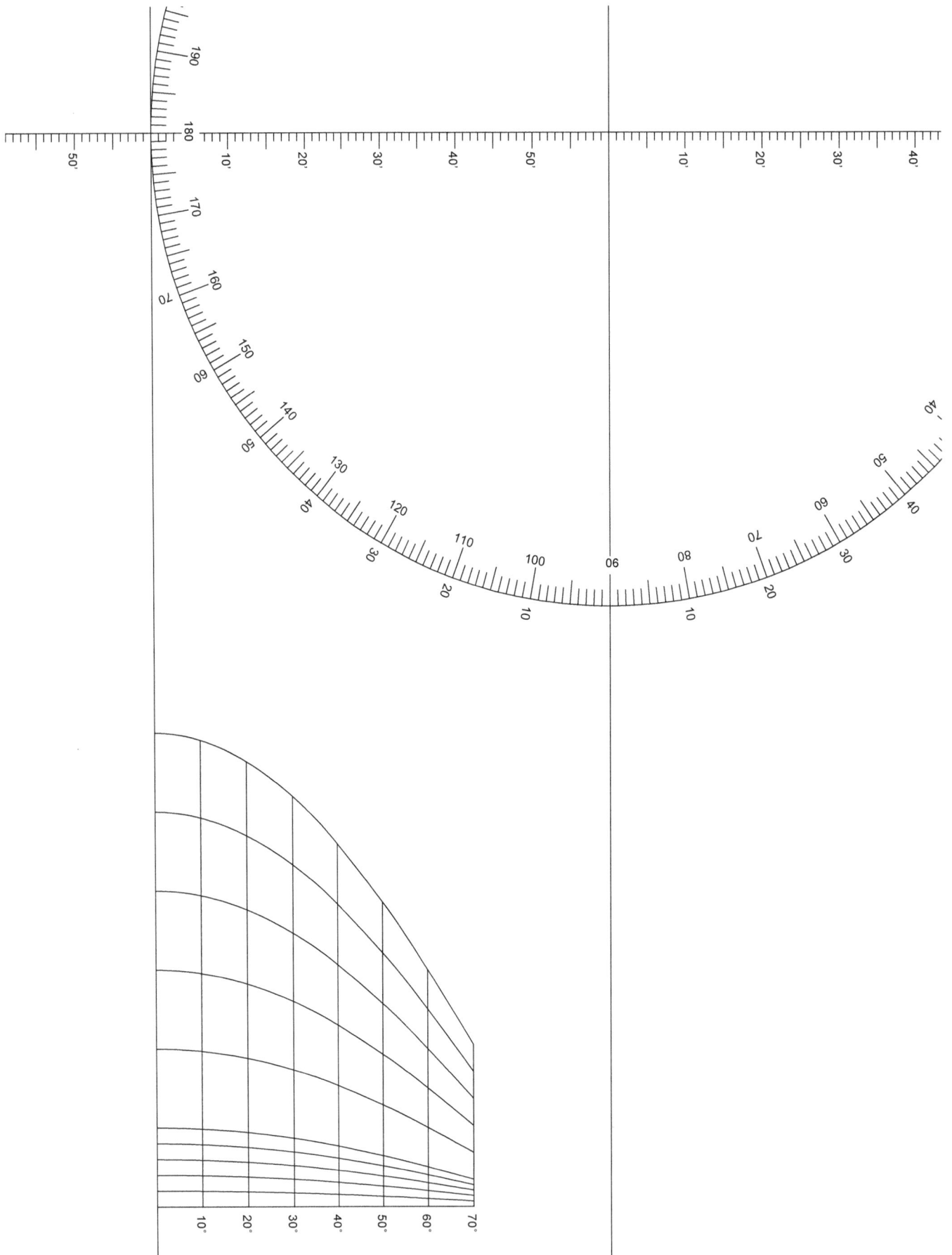

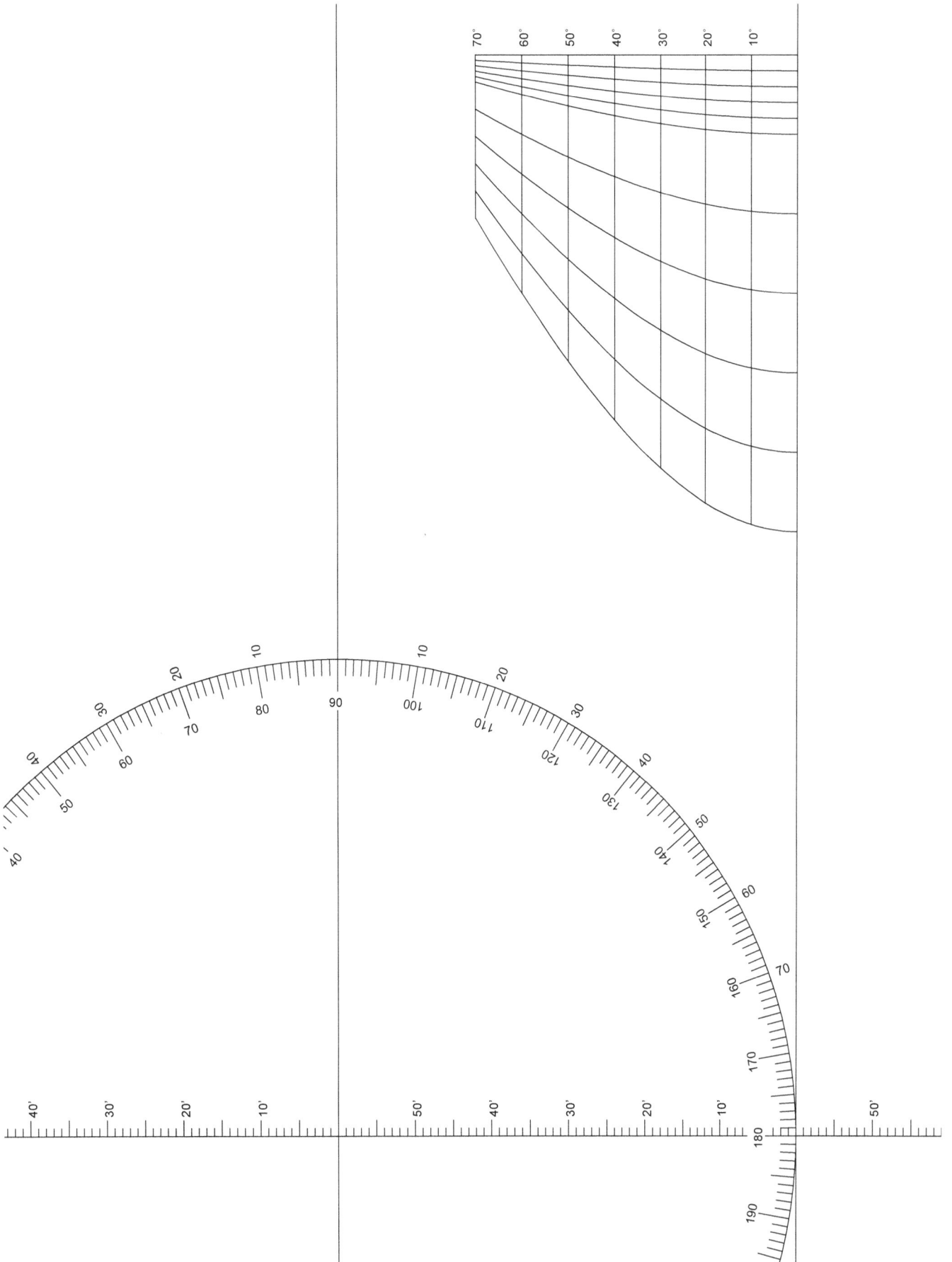

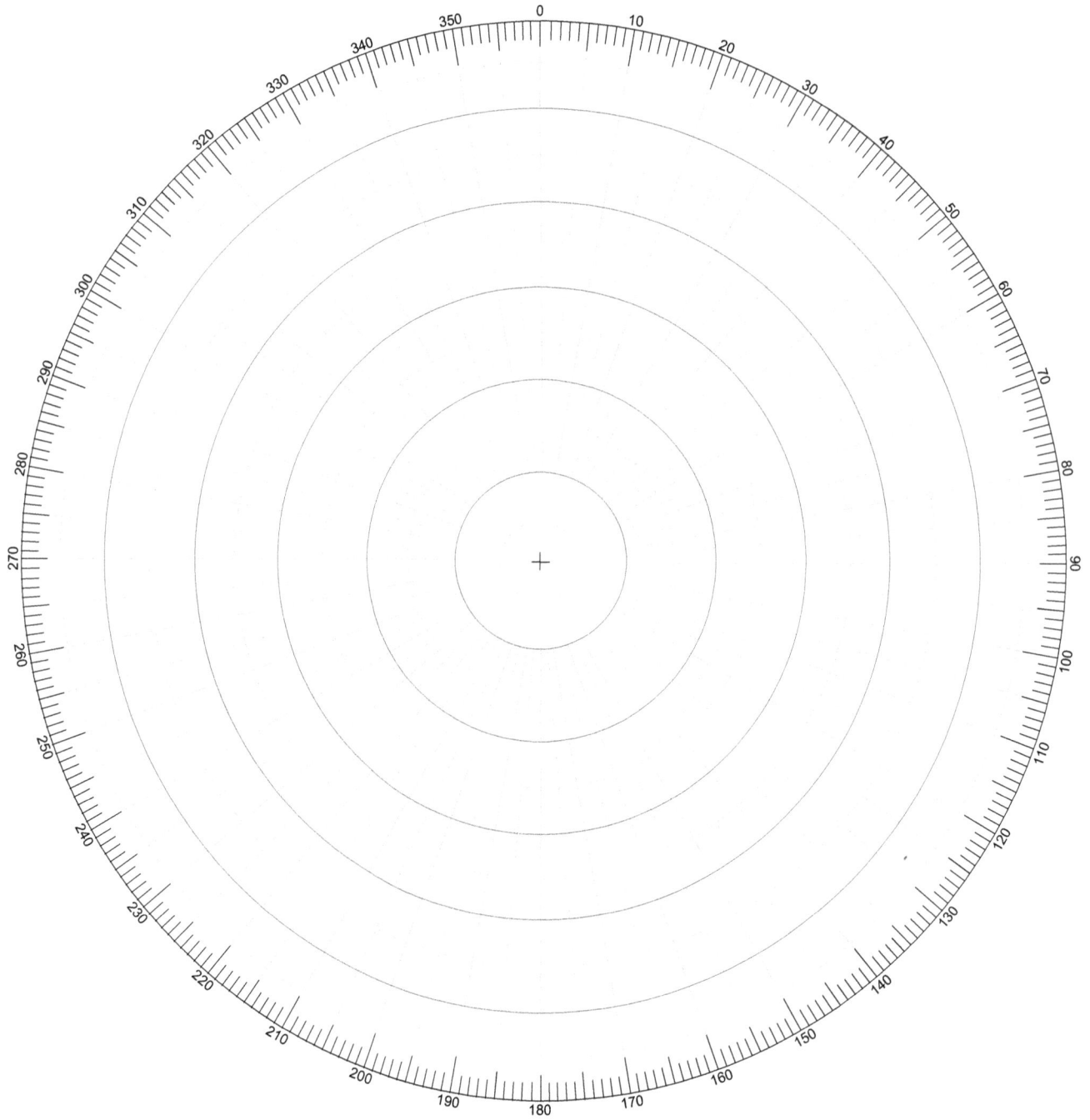

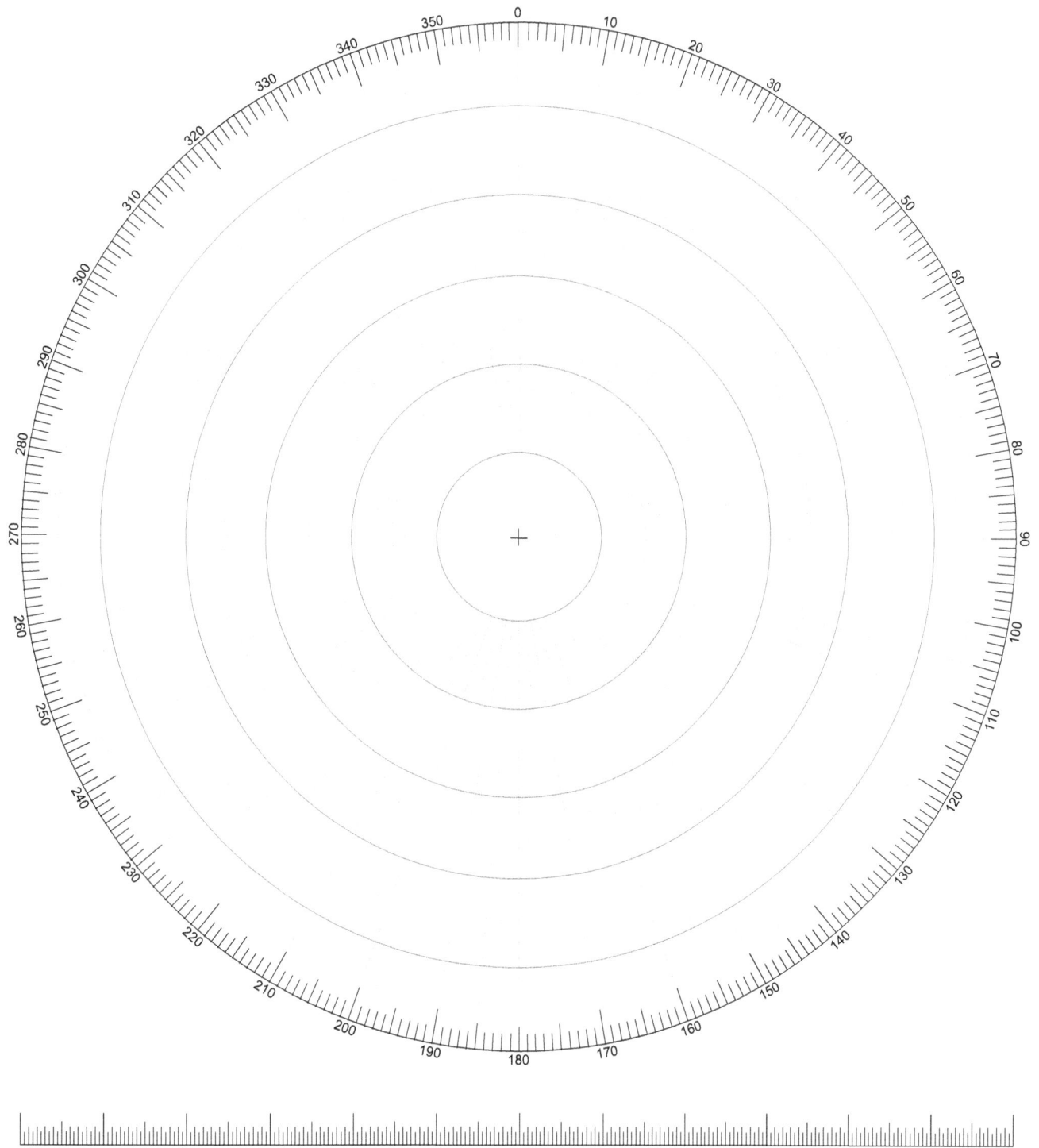

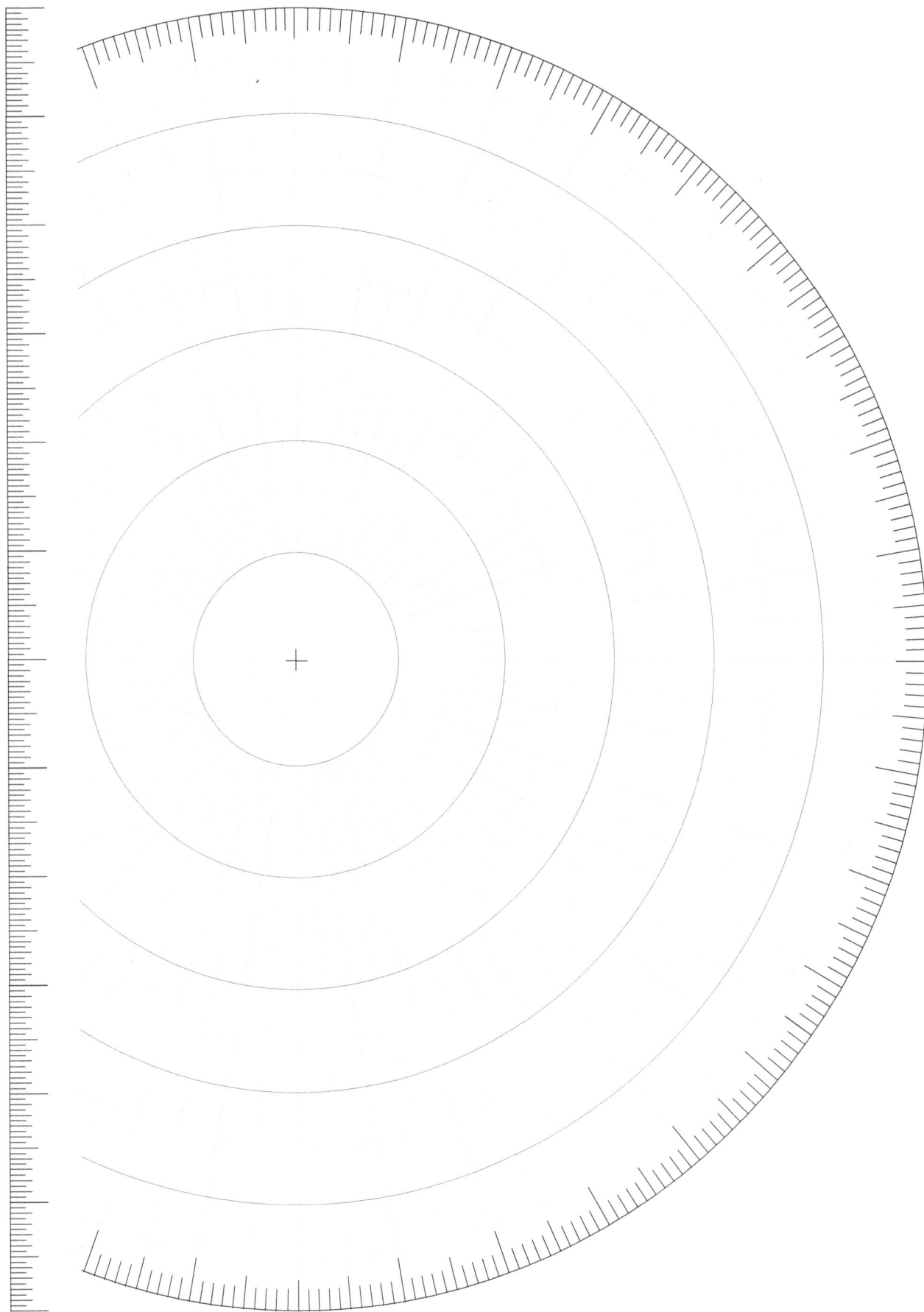

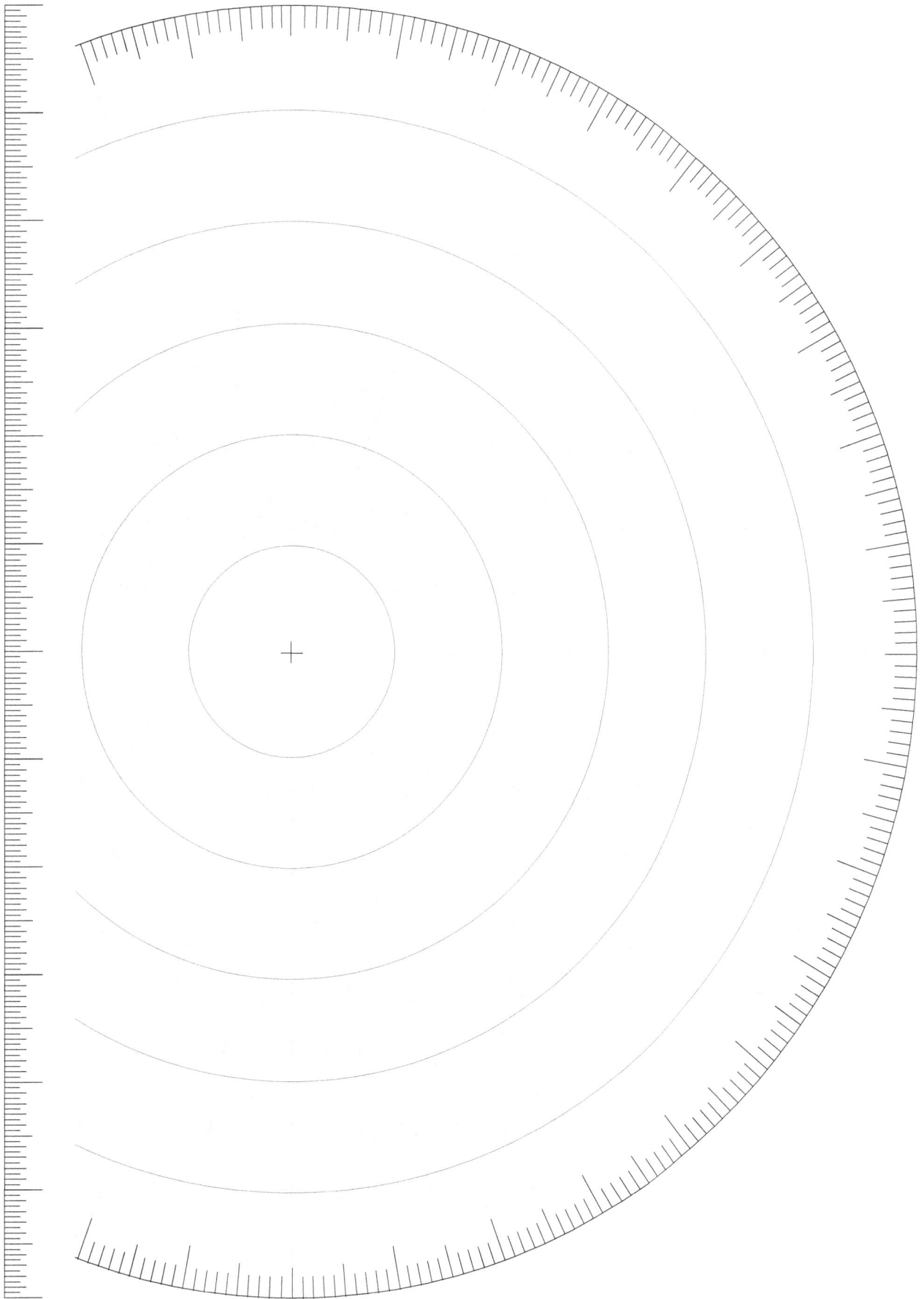

www.ingramcontent.com/pod-product-compliance
Lightning Source LLC
Chambersburg PA
CBHW080525110426
42742CB00017B/3240